Nine Ways
of
Seeing a Body

Ways of Being a Body ~ Volume 1

Nine Ways
of
Seeing a Body

Sandra Reeve

Published by:
Triarchy Press
Axminster, UK

www.triarchypress.net

First edition: 2011
Second edition: 2015
Third edition: 2021

A catalogue record for this book is available from the British Library.

Cover painting by Greta Berlin.
www.gretaberlinsculpture.com

ISBNs

Print: 978-1-908009-32-6
ePub: 978-1-908009-50-0
pdf: 978-1-908009-95-1

Dedicated to
Phillip Zarrilli
(1947-2020)

With thanks
for Phillip's spacious and alert mentorship
without which this book would not exist.

Contents

Preface

Ten years have passed since the first edition of *Nine Ways of Seeing a Body*. In that time, it has become Volume 1 of a series called 'Ways of Being a Body'.

Twenty five years ago I was living in Java, studying with Suprapto Suryodarmo at the Padepokan Lemah Putih in Solo. During practice, I had the insight that when I used the word 'body', I was talking about a process rather than a thing, and that my experience of 'body' was utterly different from that of a Javanese colleague who used the same word.

I was astonished. At that time it was already clear to me that notions of self were culturally specific and that each person's experience of self was unique; but the body still seemed so 'there' to me, so biological, anatomical, physiological, indisputable... In that moment of practice, I understood that how we view our bodies, the way we inhabit our bodies and our experience of the physiology of 'body' are equally varied and equally valid.

Around 2005, as part of my doctorate, I decided to begin to investigate different views of the body to contextualise my own work and to see how those views might have influenced my current position as a movement teacher, artist and psychotherapist engaged in movement, performance, embodiment and ecology. After all, I was constantly working with bodies ... and with attitudes.

The nine lenses that follow are the result of that investigation and are intended to be useful as a stimulus for teachers and students of dance, performance, movement, somatics, ecological thinking and the arts therapies. Perhaps they will also serve as an interdisciplinary resource for other areas of study, where a brief review of approaches to the body could be useful.

This is by no means an exhaustive study and I admit in advance to my own bias towards the somatic and ecological lenses, as these correspond with my own work and with my respect for Buddhist mindfulness practice. However, the research into overlapping aspects of the other lenses has helped me to define my own position and viewpoint along the way.

Much has moved on in our understanding of the interconnections between body, movement, mind and nature. This succinct volume offers one contribution to that field of enquiry. As information multiplies, I continue to believe that a regular personal movement practice is an irreplaceable primary source of embodied research and subsequent knowledge for all of us.

Sandra Reeve – February 2021
www.moveintolife.com

Introduction

The human body is thought about in many different ways and viewed through many different lenses. That might seem a statement of the obvious, but it is intended to offset our enduring habit of forgetting that we ever saw the world differently from the way we see it right now (whether that is 'we' as individuals, as a tribe or as a species).

Recently, it has broadly been 'situated' in eight main ways, which I describe in the pages that follow. Each lens has both been a product of its time and culture and has contributed to shaping the worldview of those who looked through it. Then I propose a ninth that, I think, both reflects our current preoccupations and might help us to address the concerns of our 21st-century world.

The eight ways or lenses are:

- the body as object

- the body as subject

- the phenomenological body

- the somatic body

- the contextual body

- the interdependent body

- the environmental body

- the cultural body

It's important to note from the outset that these lenses co-exist today: they often overlap and are not mutually exclusive. I also want to stress that this is a practitioner's account and not a purely academic explanation. The way that we experience our bodies, and how we articulate that experience, *is* of academic interest but I believe that it has also shaped – and continues to shape – our whole relationship to one another and to the world we inhabit.. That is to say, the way we in the West look at our bodies – and the sense of dislocation from our bodies that we have tended to experience – help to explain the equally dislocated worldview that has led to our current ecological crisis. Equally, in my opinion, changing the way we view our bodies can help to change the way we view the world around us and the ecosystems of which we form a part. To support those two claims, I make a twin assumption:

1. I believe that how we move shapes (and even creates) our attitudes – and reveals those attitudes to the world – to the same extent as the spoken word does.

2. I also believe that we can change our attitudes by changing our movement, provided we are aware of the dynamic interaction of our movement and the surrounding environment .

The ninth lens, which I shall explain towards the end of the book, is my developing sense of the *ecological body*, which I suggest differs from the environmental body in part because it perceives the world from motion rather than stasis. The ecological body experiences its changing self as a changing system among other environmental systems.

To bring these lenses and rather abstract ideas to life, I punctuate my analysis with a hypothetical case study that is based on my movement observation over twenty-five years. This is designed to show how I actually read movement and to signpost a way through the different lenses that I describe. Each session (in italics) recounts the progress of one individual's movement practice, as I record it in my notes. The correlation between the points made in these session notes and the text that follows it is precise. At times I make the connection explicit; otherwise I invite you to look for the connection yourself.

Lens 1: The Body as Object

F. comes into the village hall for an individual movement session. She is a photographer, aged around 55, living locally, who sees nature as one of the primary inspirations in her work. She spends most of her time outside walking and exploring different environments. She spends a lot of time alone.

When she takes a photograph, she describes herself as 'losing her body' and as focusing through her eyes, to the exclusion of sounds, which she says she does not hear. She experiences herself as being separate from the environment captured in her photographs. Instead of sensing herself as part of the situation, she feels that she positions herself in overview.

She has two aims in engaging in movement practice. The first is to develop a more embodied approach to her photography. She hopes that this will influence the sense of rhythm and involved participation in her photographs. The second is to 'keep her body flexible', as she is worried about getting stiffer in the joints, and the fact that she has pain developing in her right shoulder.

....

> I thereby concluded that I was a substance, of
> which the whole essence or nature consists in
> thinking, and which, in order to exist, needs no
> place and depends on no material thing; so that
> this 'I', that is to say, the mind, by which I am
> what I am is entirely distinct from the body, and
> even that it is easier to know than the body, and
> moreover, that even if the body were not, it would
> not cease to be all that is.
>
> René Descartes, *Discourse on Method, 54*

These words of René Descartes, written in 1637, set in motion the whole idea of the 'body as object', which is also referred to as the mechanistic body. In Cartesian thought, the body was seen as an inert object, facilitating the needs and desires of the mind, which could exist independently.

Philosophically, this position has now been largely abandoned. However, it still informs the major part of Western daily-life practice and is promoted not least by orthodox (allopathic) medicine, which remains a primary influence on our daily-life attitudes to our own bodies. For example, in the face of the ageing process, we are often encouraged to strive to remain young and to overcome our changing physical capacities, rather than acknowledging change and allowing ourselves to be stimulated into new possibilities, compatible with the capabilities of our individual bodies now.

Heward Wilkinson, in his introduction to a series of essays on the embodied mind in psychotherapy, points to all kinds of commodification of the body. He discusses, for example, the perfect body – which is to be achieved through diet and certain kinds of exercise – and he talks about how the body is replacing dreams as the seat of the unconscious in psychotherapy. Both these examples reveal an approach that *does* give some value to the body as a resource. However, it is also an approach that tends to view the body as an object that we do something to, or as a container that provides us with information for our conscious life, rather than as an intrinsic part of our being and of our sense of self.

The Cartesian approach, in its assumption of a disembodied mind, has been associated with a particular view of knowledge that is closely linked to mind and to the sense of sight. The mind seems connected to sight, gazing down at an unintelligent object called body that operates through the other classical senses of smell, touch, taste and hearing, as well as the kinaesthetic sense. Smell, taste, hearing and touch invite experiences of immersion and a fluidity between boundaries, whereas sight encourages a sense of distance and clear boundary, for example when we close our eyes. According to Jerri Daboo:

> Sight is the sense of the separate observer (the 'I'),
> and of the disembodied mind. For Descartes, who
> believed that human essence is only found in the
> mind and not the body, 'the sense of science was to
> be sight'... and so sight is separated from the body,
> and placed in a superior position to it.

An observer seeing from disembodied mind, looking at the world 'out there' through her eyes, will tend to see anything 'other' as an object, including her own and other bodies. Each object will, in turn, be seen to have a clear boundary.

The primacy given to the sense of sight, combined with the discovery of perspective as a Western aesthetic, has created distance between the position of the subject and the object. Perspective has profoundly influenced our consciousness, so that we have the sense of a separate self, a fixed point looking into the distance, situated outside the environment we are looking at, as if it were a painting or a landscape. John Dewey makes the connection between this fixed point of vision and fixed objects, when we imagine that we are uninvolved observers of the world:

> The theory of knowing is modelled after what
> we suppose to take place in the act of vision.
> The object refracts light to the eye and is seen; it

> makes a difference to the eye and to the person
> having an optical apparatus, but none to the thing
> seen. The real object is the object so fixed in its
> regal aloofness that it is a king to any beholding
> mind that may gaze upon it. A spectator theory of
> knowledge is the inevitable outcome.

This 'spectator theory of knowledge', linked to sight and perspective, has given rise to the modern notion of individualism. If I am a mere spectator, then I am not responsible for the events that I am witnessing, and I have no motivation to consider (that is, to be self-reflexive about) my contribution to the situation.

This particular notion of individualism is experientially challenged by ecological movement practice (described in more detail later in this book), which places visual perception as just one of the senses involved in the continuum of the moving being in a moving environment. In ecological movement practice, as I move, I try to be aware through all my senses of my changing position in a changing environment, rather than prioritising my visual sense as a static and objective source of information about a supposedly static and objectified environment.

Lens 2: The Body as Subject

I suggest to F. that she begin her practice by walking in any variation: walking, running, skipping, hopping and paying attention to how she places her feet as she moves.

Does she have the sensation of landing or taking off from the ground when she moves?

Is she 'late' in bringing her back foot through, which would restrain her walk, or is her intention in time with the rhythm of her walk?

As a contrast to her professional visual orientation, I suggest that she pay attention to the sounds she can hear around her and that she allow her eyes to follow, rather than to lead, her movement. I suggest that in this period of practice her eyes should be in passive mode, seeing what is there, rather than looking for something specific.

As she begins to move, I move in the space too, aware of the impact and the atmosphere of her movement in the environment, so that she has a sense of participation – rather than of being looked at – by me. Gradually, as she becomes involved in the task and more confident, I move to the side of the room and witness her work without losing my own awareness of sound. Her eyes are still very active and directing her movement, so I invite her to explore different points, lines and angles of view as she moves.

Puzzled, she starts to experiment with changing the position of her head to change her viewpoint in standing, lying, sitting and crawling; the rest of her body follows in movement. At this point her movement reveals her growing awareness that her sense of sight is connected to her head, neck and spine. I ask her to relax her eyes as she moves. Her movement softens as she realises how tired her eyes are. I remind her to become aware of the sounds in the room and she continues to move.

She comments later that, as she relaxed her eyes, she felt like a huge weight was lifting off her, and that she could begin to enjoy her movement in relation to the soundscape, without constantly searching for meaning.

•••••••••••••••••••••••••••••

It can be difficult to step back and see how strongly our culture is influenced by these notions of the primacy of sight, of the primary connection between sight and knowledge, of objects as independent units and of the necessity for an objective, and therefore detached, stance. Non-stylised movement challenges all these notions. It is intended to be (and is) accessible to all, encouraging an attitude of participation. The source of non-stylised movement is daily life and movement practice supports the emergence of an individual's movement vocabulary that is 'in-formed' by their own unique body. It can also be one of the foundation stones for dance/theatre performance, where participants from both traditions seek to work together to create a performance.

Taking the latter example for a moment, if we look back at the development of physical theatre, Peter Brook, Jerzy Grotowski and Eugenio Barba can all be seen to have used physicality and movement to challenge the primacy of sight, the notion of audience as distanced observer and the monopoly of text–based theatre. The training methods that they used concentrated on releasing blocks in the physical body and voice, rather than accumulating formal acting skills in order to demonstrate meaning. For example, the approach of Grotowski's *via negativa* enabled spontaneous and appropriate physical acts to occur through improvisation. These were then re-worked into a performance score. The idea of the audience as separated observers gave way to experiments where the audience was placed as witness or participant or given a specific role to play, such as being guests invited to dine at the 'last supper' of Doctor Faustus.

These devices evoked for the audience embodied experiences that involved all the senses through participation or through approaches known as immersion or communion. These trends, which may be seen as attempts to include the audience fully as part of an experience, have continued to the present day and include promenade, site-specific performance and ecological performance, which foreground environment and the position of the audience as participating elements in the performance. They all challenge the habit of thinking about performance as an observed event.

With the advent of two distinct disciplines, phenomenology and somatics, attention shifted to valuing the subjective experience of the body and our experience in the body. One distinction between them is that phenomenology approaches notions of 'mind and body as one being' from the view of mind, while somatic studies approach them from the view of body. Non-stylised movement creates a broad enough practice for these two starting points to be explored and acknowledged in turn, through self-reflexive and experiential movement dialogue. A mover can start moving from thoughts or from body structure, or indeed from feelings. Where the attention is placed as I move reveals my attitude and my preferred way of accessing the world. At some point, through awareness, exploration and enlivening all the senses in the environment, movement integrates thoughts with feelings and with physical sensations. In this way I gradually develop an embodied movement vocabulary.

Heward Wilkinson touches on the same distinction between thought and physical sensation, but interestingly, as is the prevalent habit in the 'body-mind' debate, does not refer to a specific approach from feeling. He sees the distinction as 'a difference in metaphysical approach' and attributes what I have described here as a 'view from body' to the lineage of 'realist materialists who would say that the experienced body is totally dependant on the physical body' and what I have described here as a 'view from the mind' as belonging to 'those who start from a substantially, or primarily spirit-centred position (such as most of the humanistic, transpersonal, Jungian, body psychotherapy based positions)'.

Specifically, to understand the 'view from body', we can look at the anti-reductionist approach taken by Jaak Panksepp in his neuroscientific research on the mammalian brain and, to understand the 'view from mind', we can look at the Jungian approach to the experienced body.

Feelings, which are discussed in Lens 6, are now playing a role in drawing together these two different approaches. This convergence is seen in self-reflexive movement practice, where an awareness of the shifting flux of thoughts, physical sensations and feelings is part of a relational practice of becoming-within-the-environment.

Lens 3: The Phenomenological Body

I had given F. a clear physical task and directed her attention to an unfamiliar sense (hearing) to guide her movement. Her preference for the visual sense was initially too strong for her to prioritise hearing. In response, I gave her a physical task which connected to vision, but which challenged the ways she usually looked, demanding unfamiliar positions. As her experience of sight and physical structure became more integrated, I asked her to relax her eyes, which also led her to relax her trying – literally, her focus. From there, she was able to begin to include the sounds and also to become aware of her feelings.

This is an example of her movement starting from an idea, and gradually integrating the body and feelings (a phenomenological approach). By asking F. to pay attention to her senses in relation to movement, she becomes aware of both the watcher and the watched, the hearer and the heard. The process would have been utterly different if she had responded to the first task of paying attention to her feet, by closing her eyes and responding to touch, texture and the articulation of her joints in movement (a somatic approach). I would have read this as an affinity with initiating movement from structure and would have waited to see which of the sensory worlds was more accessible to her from that position: sound or vision. My experience would suggest that opening her eyes would then have been the final step, once she had integrated structure with responding to outer and inner sounds through movement.

. . . .

> Whereas psychology studies actual subjective
> responses to actual environmental events
> (empirical data), phenomenology studies the
> essential character of consciousness in meaning-
> conferring acts (essential knowledge)… In
> summary, then, Husserl's overall program of
> phenomenology sought to clarify our implicit
> preunderstandings of the world.

In Lens 2, we encountered the phenomenological and the somatic approach to the body and to our experience in the body and saw that phenomenology engages with notions of body-mind from the viewpoint of mind, while somatic studies do so from the viewpoint of body. Putting attention on the source of a discipline, as well as on the resulting insights, can allow practitioners to become aware of their own attraction to certain words and ways of working. Phenomenology refers to 'body image' and 'body schema', but it analyses both of these from the viewpoint of mind. The somatic approach of Moshe Feldenkrais refers to 'self-image' and 'structure and function', but it touches on both of these from the viewpoint of body.

An existential, phenomenological approach to body-mind emphasises what is immediately felt and experienced by human beings. This approach requires us to think about and consider our own awareness and our subjective experience (including our subjective experience of that awareness), particularly as we experience it through physical sensations.

Phenomenologists are interested in the experience of 'knowing' rather than 'knowing about' and in the human capacity for self-reflexivity (which is to say our capacity for reflecting on and about our own experiences, thoughts, sensations, feelings and internal processes). In order to analyse subjective experiences, phenomenologists give attention to key motifs that emerge from our accounts of our own experiences. Key motifs in a shared event are the aspects of the experience that cannot be changed without fundamentally altering the narrative of the event. Individual key motifs may be seen to reflect and reveal the particular quality of a person's 'intentionality' in consciousness, emphasised by Edmund Husserl (1859–1938) as the way in which consciousness is always pointing towards something:

> …consciousness can therefore serve as an
> 'object' for itself. Hence, one can be conscious of
> consciousness itself, 'intending' emotions, desires,
> and other states of conscious experience.

Phenomenological analysis is often combined with other related perspectives, such as existentialism, which is also based in subjective experience, but focuses on the dynamic quality of human existence, seeing people as always in the process of 'becoming', rather than as fixed entities, and therefore takes as given the fact of constant change.

For phenomenologists, the 'lived body' is:

> …presented not as a representable object but
> in the immediacy of its lived concreteness.
> The experienced body is not an object for the
> abstractive gaze: it is the body *as lived, as lodged*
> *in the world* as a base of operations from which
> attitudes are assumed and projects deployed.

When examining bodily phenomena, Maurice Merleau-Ponty argued that the body is experienced as *both* body-subject and body-object. He suggests that we should examine 'consciousness itself as a project of the world, meant for a world which it neither embraces, nor possesses, but towards which it is permanently directed'. This attitude acknowledges a dynamic between perceiver and perceived, a condition amplified in movement practice. This shift of emphasis to the role of perception in consciousness is one that we will come back to later in relation to movement and ecological perception.

Merleau-Ponty also argued that meaning cannot be attributed to ideas alone, but that there is an inherent meaning in materiality (in things). For example, he noted that if a painting is torn up, it no longer has meaning but is returned to strips of canvas; whereas if one breaks up a stone, the pieces that remain are still pieces of stone. 'The real is distinguishable from our fictions because in reality the significance encircles and permeates matter'.

In relation to movement, meaning is often attributed to the body through the interpretation or assumptions of the mind, whether that is the mind of the mover or the mind of the witness. This is consistent with a phenomenological approach. But I would argue that the materiality of the body alive in movement holds its own 'meaning', which expresses itself in time and space. It can tell the fact of its own distinct existence and changing nature through movement; movement can also evoke multiple (and immediate) sensed interpretations. This approach takes us towards the somatic body.

Lens 4: The Somatic Body

I ask F. to pay attention to how she places her feet as she moves. Once she becomes involved in her practice, I ask her to practise going down to the ground, crawling in any variation, and coming back up into walking, as simply as possible, paying attention to how her body structure fulfils those sequences. I notice the amount of tension or release in her movement at any given moment, whether she prefers to be up or down, how she pushes or pulls her body through various movements, which parts of the sequence she seems most comfortable in. She seems reluctant to relax her body weight onto the ground.

From time to time I ask her to stop, to hold her position and to relax any unnecessary tension in her muscles and joints, without changing the physical shape of her body. After a few moments, I ask her to carry on, and I notice which part of her body initiates the movement. Occasionally I encourage her not to hold her breath.

....

Somatic studies begin from the sense of meaning inherent in materiality. The body structure becomes inherently meaningful as it develops attitudinal patterns through engaging with environmental factors and other bodies. As a rapidly developing field of studies in dance, psychology, psychotherapy, performance, bodywork and anthropology, somatic studies begin from a sensorimotoric functional approach to how the body engages with its environment and from what Janet Eddy calls, "… 'listening to the body' and responding to these sensations by consciously altering movement habits and movement choices".

As a general approach, in systems such as Feldenkrais, Somatics and Body-Mind Centering (BMC), a client is guided to track physical sensations or shapes, to gradually become conscious of the movements and positions that are already present and to release any block or held pattern that may be a root cause of the difficulties in their present situation.

In evolutionary and developmental movement systems such as BMC, physical exercises are given to develop body awareness, which is the capacity to pay attention with and through the body to the flux of physical and felt sensations. The individual is then helped through touch and words to consciously explore and re-shape the particular movements that preceded the area of developmental difficulty: for example crawling may be reinvestigated as the vocabulary prior to the transition to standing up. This process is seen as providing the body with a strong enough base to release the block that has developed as a result of a kinaesthetic weakness.

In Somatics and Feldenkrais, subtle levels of movement are explored and emphasis is placed on providing the individual client with a wider choice of movement possibilities and on releasing fixed habits, so that the body can select new and more appropriate options for dealing with specific environmental tasks. The body is seen as able to select the best possible route for the task in hand, for example lifting a heavy suitcase, once the nervous system has been reminded of its options through guided movements. According to these systems, there is neither a correct nor incorrect way of moving *per se*.

In somatic practice, or moving from the view of body, I encourage the individual to become aware of the structure of the living body in movement.

At a structural level, I find it useful to look at what has been termed by Janet Kaylo, movement analyst and founder of the Laban/Bartenieff & Somatic Studies International Institute, as: 'inner space' processes, 'body-level' processes, (which are visible where the boundary of the body meets the external space) and 'outer space/kinaesphere' processes. Examples of 'inner space' processes include breathing or noticing from where the performer initiates or organises their movement sequences. 'Body-level' processes include noticing boundaries in the body's connectivity, for example which areas of the body specifically push outward, or collapse inwardly in relation to bony landmarks such as the head, scapulae, sternum, ilia and heels. 'Kinaesphere processes' reveal how each person manifests patterns in their movement sequences, through the way in which they use space through developmental patterning, such as spatial intent, e.g. Reach and Push/Pull. This particular deconstruction of the body in movement allows me to notice whether I am paying more attention to the inner landscape of the person, to the outer environment or to the interface between the two, at any given moment.

I pay attention to how individuals combine in their movement the different Laban Efforts: flow, weight, space and time. For example, in terms of 'space', if invited to move in a room, paying attention to the feet, one person will gradually reveal a preference for walking in straight lines, or around the extremity of the room rather than through the middle. Another will enjoy moving in curves and circles, rarely stopping and constantly changing level in the space: standing, crawling, rolling. Yet another will never leave the floor but will pay meticulous attention to the placing of the soles of their feet as they engage with a variety of different modes of crossing the space. The variations are endless and literally incomparable.

In terms of 'time', (which includes rhythm), participants also reveal temporal preferences: moving swiftly and then long pauses; always arriving first in the group but always speaking last; slow movement that gradually builds to a crescendo, but at the last minute returns to a slow tempo; dragging the back foot which holds them back, in terms of following through impulses in the body. In terms of 'weight', participants often appear to have selected particular ranges that suit them through the spectrum of being very light to very heavy on their feet or in their positions in space. In terms of 'flow', which corresponds to how tense or relaxed the mover is, movement varies from toned to tense to collapsed or relaxed: although there may be variation, each individual usually returns repeatedly to one quality within each effort as a base where they feel most 'at home' or seem to recognize themselves.

I witness these personal preferences and variations from a consideration of how each individual can give themselves more choices in how they move. For example, tasks I set participants include noticing how they place their feet on the ground. Do they put more weight on their heel or the ball of their foot? Do they emphasise landing on the ground, or taking off from the ground? How does this affect their attitude? Do they tend to ask questions (lifting off) or make statements (landing)? Do they prefer to arrive into (landing) or leave (taking off) a situation? Does this correspond with a kinaesthetic preference for landing or taking off? Playing with alternative types of step widens the choice of movement vocabulary and possible attitudes. Participants are encouraged to give all movements equal value.

My intention is to accept and appreciate what they can already do and to help them to clarify their own particular habits, so that they can become aware of how they move (their own unique movement vocabulary). This amplification and definition of their choice of patterns gradually helps people to be bodily aware of how they do, *as they are doing it*, rather than retrospectively, or not at all – and to cultivate acceptance as the first stage of transformation.

Participants push, pull and are pushed and pulled, through different surfaces of the body. These actions contract and release muscle groups and stimulate the body to remember patterns of early developmental movement. They also reveal whether the characteristic tendency is to push away (averse), to hold on to (acquisitive) or either to shift rapidly between pushing away and holding on, or 'freeze' (confused), faced with a person, object or situation. Students are taken through moving each joint, to explore flexibility and to demonstrate how to expand the range of possible movements within their own limitations. Gradually, by moving through the musculoskeletal system, students become aware of which parts of the body feel familiar and which areas feel unknown. Personal meaning or interpretation emerges of its own accord from this kind of rigorous structural investigation.

Finally, participants are taught how to 'follow their line' through movement. Here students are encouraged to move as they wish, but to follow the sequence of physical sensations of their body in movement. Initially the task may be to name the objects of their shifting attention as they move, as simply as possible: knee, floor, cold, stretch, hand, thought, etc. This helps to integrate thoughts, perception and movement. Or, without words, they may be encouraged to bring into their movement whatever their experience is at the time: if they feel heat, to express it; if they are attracted by sounds, to respond through movement; if they find themselves thinking, to embody the sensation of 'thinking' in their movement.

At times they may be invited to explore the sensation or the impulse by amplifying it in movement. This exaggeration can create a caricature, which both promotes humour and serves to relax identification with the pattern. At times it is useful to slow the sequence of movement down, maintaining a sustained flow. Participants can then sense more easily how, as they embody a feeling, a thought or a physical sensation (whichever is foregrounded at that moment), they are weaving an intricate web of action and response in the environment around them. This kinaesthetic perception supports an attitude of participation in, and co-creation of, a situation, rather than a sense of being central to a situation that is happening *to* them.

Lens 5: The Contextual Body

Gradually F. finds fluidity within the task of moving from up to down and crawling in between. I notice that, unless I ask her to stop, she is constantly moving, often repeating and reiterating the same circular pathways in the hall. She moves around the outside of the room, or in a small circle in the centre of the room. She rarely moves in straight lines. I ask her to find her own pauses, without feeling as if she is breaking her flow, or losing a sense of fluidity. I suggest that she could just pause in her sequence, relax and then continue. At the end of the session she comments that she feels more comfortable on the ground now, although at the beginning she felt as if being on the ground was unsafe because she lost her sense of overview. She also comments that in her daily life, she never stops to take a rest, because there is never enough time and she is afraid that she will lose her thread. At the end of the day she is utterly exhausted. She was reminded of that pattern in her practice and could begin to see how it might influence her contact with friends and colleagues.

....

As we have seen, a fundamental aspect of the phenomenological body is the attention given to the human capacity for self-reflexivity as a result of contact with the mover's surrounding environment, including other people.

Somatic practices explore an individual's characteristic tendencies through bodywork or movement and, from there, comment on the influence those habits can have on environmental and cultural issues. Don Hanlon Johnson looks for a 'technology of authenticity', commenting that:

> Dualism is the way in which we are trained to move, perceive and feel. [...] We can't loosen its grip on our muscles simply by rational analysis. Authenticity means to do something oneself, to have a sense that one's actions and feelings are one's own. [...] Training is vital to become aware that his or her worldly behaviour is indeed theirs and has consequences.

By interrupting this dualistic training, we can bring our intentions and actions up to date, so that our movement embodies our own unique perceptions and subsequent actions. Somatics makes clear that the individual organism is related to the whole system.

As our detailed neuroscientific knowledge of the body expands, it feels important to remember to articulate the significance of connectivity, community and thus the role of context within a predominantly non-verbal style of work. Amanda Williamson is also explicit in talking about the skills that a somatic approach can offer to social environments, for example 'the internalization of authority, self-awareness, self-knowledge, and self-education', and the capacity to become 'active agents in our experience, sensually alive, and co-actively engaged with our world.'

So whether from 'the view of mind' or from 'the view of body', the individual's subjective lived experience is considered in relationship to its context, in the broadest sense: the familial, social and cultural environments as well as the natural environment.

Somatic practitioners are trained in the perception of minimal movements and flow in relation to the body moving through the environment. Bainbridge Cohen has given a useful example of starting from the perception of the body, in order to witness the interplay of body-mind-environment, rather than starting from a philosophical or psychological idea and seeing how the body's activity supports that philosophy.

> There is something in nature that forms patterns.
> We as part of nature also form patterns. The mind
> is like the wind and the body like the sand: if you
> want to know how the wind is blowing, you look
> at the sand. […] I think that all mind patternings
> are expressed in movement through the body. And
> that all physically moving patterns have a mind.
> That's what I work with. […] Patterns that exist in
> the world outside the body exist also in the world
> inside the body.

In my case study, there is an example of challenging a particular pattern by offering an alternative. (*F. never stops in her movement; I suggest finding pauses.*) The student develops those observations into a broader field of relevance. (*F.'s commentary on her rhythms in her daily life.*) In terms of patterns, I noticed how she preferred to move in circles, either around the edge of the room or in the middle, but I chose to prioritise working with her stopping. I see this habitual use of space as an example of a 'mind patterning', and work through movement to give awareness of the movement pattern and to stimulate other possible relationships to environmental space. This can all happen without the need for my interpretation of what that pattern means for the mover, although that information may come to light for them.

Through my own training in *Joged Amerta* with the Javanese movement artist Suprapto Suryodarmo, I have learnt to identify whether individuals are more likely to access the world primarily through their sensory experience of light (vision), sound (hearing) or touch (body). This I do by observing how their movement is influenced by the environment and also by listening to their description of their practice. Given the choice, some analyse their movement by giving reasons for what they did, which would indicate a mental approach. Others work through images, describing their pictorial experience of the inner story. They often decipher its personal symbolic significance at the same time, from a feeling approach. Others have a physical approach, describing the thread of their physical actions/activities. This unravelling tends to reveal its own meaning to them.

If I am self-reflexive about whether I tend to initiate my movement primarily from my body, my mind or my feelings, as well as conscious of the preferences revealed by the source of a psychophysical discipline I am engaging with, this gives me the ground to identify and appreciate the primary source of other disciplines working in the same field. It is usual to examine the aim or goal of a particular psychophysical practice, but perhaps paying attention to the source of different psychophysical disciplines – 'where they are coming from' – may help to avoid misunderstandings and conflicts between practitioners and cultures. Each articulated approach is relative rather than contradictory to another approach. In the selected examples of phenomenology and somatics, although each may be seen as initiating research from opposite ends of the spectrum, we can also see that they are not contradictory but relative and may benefit from recognising each other's difference and working in dialogue with each other, rather than seeking a compromise or a synthesis.

Lens 6: The Interdependent Body

F. has been practising moving from up to down and crawling and also exploring different physical viewpoints in relation to her photography. I decide to do a guiding session.

We begin to move, each paying attention to ourselves. Once involved in movement, I suggest that we become aware of our surroundings: I notice the textures of the wooden floor, chairs and beams, the iron of the bell, the radiator, the glass of the windows with the leaves beyond. She notices the play of light and shadow on the walls, reads the notices on the walls, walks around the edge of the room, looking into the centre and looking out of the windows. As I pay attention to her movement, to her mood and to the atmosphere around her, I begin to move in a staccato rhythm, my fingers come alive making shapes and signs. I point with different fingers; the whole of my body follows the line of gesture and then releases into the next movement.

I notice F. responding to the suggestions that I am shaping in the space. She explores moving her fingers, bending her knees a little so that the movement initiated from her fingertips can travel right through her body to her feet. She laughs and dances faster, her capacity for focus no longer held fixed, but integrated in a rhythmic dance of points. Her shoulders release a little, particularly her right shoulder, as she stretches her arm out in all directions. As she goes down to the ground, she continues to articulate her fingers, pointing to patches of sunlight and tracing the line of a shadow on the ground.

During this time I have quietly been supporting whatever she is doing through the quality of my own movement, in terms of rhythm, weight or use of space. I now stop and remain a present witness to her closing movement. It is time for her to act on her own now. She pauses, the rhythm slows down and she traces the outline of her own hand, thoughtfully stretching and releasing her fingers, running her finger up the inside of her arm until she is pointing at her own breastbone. She finds herself looking straight at a notice that says 'The Breath of Life' (advertising an event in the hall the following week). She smiles, breathes deeply and relaxes into her position.

....

As with the previous lens, the interdependent body continues the process of incorporating the view from body and the view from mind. A precise example of this convergence in body movement is offered by Elizabeth Behnke, a phenomenologist who explores a somatic exercise called matching through a phenomenological lens. She describes the phenomenon of matching as a way of entering into the exact shape of a held pattern in one's own body and maintaining it through time, which, she argues, 'possibilizes' other dynamic options.

> Matching is a way of overcoming ingrained
> dualism; it involves a dynamic and participatory
> appreciation of time, it is predicated on a tendency
> towards health and wholeness, it encourages
> autonomy and responsibility without isolating
> the individual from the context [...] Matching,
> however, is a way of re-appropriating my body
> as me [...] with matching then, it is as though I
> begin to melt the boundary that the I-It paradigm

> imposes between me and my own body, and I can
> begin to let me-ness flow more fully into the whole
> of me.

In this way, notions of body as a subject or body as an object merge into one dynamic experience of I/me-in-movement, which is continuous through time and holds within it the capacity for change. By engaging through movement with a held pattern that I have identified, I am both initiating a movement but also receiving the result of that movement through sensations as I 'match' myself, in a continuous feedback loop. The task provides an opportunity for me to re-enter freshly a reiterative pattern that has become my particular norm and, by that action, to interrupt it so that it can change.

> Matching means that something static is
> transformed into something that on-goingly
> continues to be just this way. And habitual shapes
> are habitual precisely because they are reiterated.
> With matching I get inside the skin of the
> reiteration.

Matching can transform the fixed notion of time that exists as part of a held physical pattern. In this way, a fixed notion of time contributes to a fixed sense of self. A pattern does not have to be 'forever': it is constellated in this on-going moment through interwoven factors, and can shift if the contributing factors change.

Matching is a passive approach to bodywork, by which I mean that it relies on listening, being patient and acceptance rather than starting from doing, having a goal and trying to change a pattern through manipulation. The matching principle can also be applied with a client. Hanna calls this kinetic mirroring, where the body worker, using touch, 'goes with', follows or matches a particular shape or movement that the client's body likes to make, either by maintaining it through holding the position or, if it is a movement, slowing it right down so that the change of rhythm interrupts the client's sensorimotoric amnesia. This offers opportunities for change.

As we look at somatic experience through the lens of interdependence and interconnectivity, it is clear that we are who we are because of our location within a broader pattern and because of our interconnection with one another and with larger wholes. Here, we can also consider interspecies somatic dialogue.

Matching, for Behnke, as well as for somatic practitioners, takes place without explicit attention to the environment. In my own work, a convergence between a phenomenological and somatic approach to body occurs through the practice of guiding. Guiding is a way of teaching movement through moving. I use it to teach movement by moving with the participant with an awareness of context and 'environmentally' (in outdoor locations), rather than through tasks or verbal instruction. It is like matching in the attitudes that it adopts, but it is a more active and consciously participatory approach that includes environmental awareness.

I begin by paying attention to my own body movement, become aware of my movement *in the environment* and then to the student's movement *as part of the environment*. As I move, I receive the atmosphere of the other mover through all my senses and then allow myself to respond to their 'landscape' through movement in the role of guiding. At this time, I am aware of our surroundings and of us as movers, constantly changing and shifting position. I experience life consciously from the view of transition, with static positions as part of that never ending flow, and with both moving bodies and identities in a rapport of co-creation. I cannot say that I am teaching from that position, but I am introducing movement stimuli into a dynamic situation which I am part of: an approach that I consider to be relevant and beneficial for the development of the other mover. My experience shows that if a stimulus is useful or relevant, the other mover will notice it and incorporate it into his/her movement.

Behnke's phenomenological analysis is helpful as a framework for speaking about work based in sensation. However, she herself recognizes the gap between the somatic approach and her own analysis, when she says that her writing is a phenomenological explanation of the process of matching. She clarifies that a somatics practitioner would only be satisfied if that description were complemented by a biological account of the processes involved, thus demonstrating a recognition not just of the difference between the two disciplines, but of the need to respect the different ways of speaking about them. Later in this book I talk about what I perceive as an ecological body, which speaks from within the flux of change rather than from a fixed, static position and which honours the many layers of that body-in-the-environment's experience through movement.

I have already mentioned the absence of a position for 'feelings' in the body-mind debate. Current neuroscientific research seems to be not only providing a bridge between the parallel processes of somatic research and psychological/philosophical enquiry, but also introducing a respectable basis for understanding feelings. Neuroscience continues to illuminate the convergence of body, mind and perception as interwoven processes, as much as quantum physics previously affected our notions of matter, motion and field. In general terms, mind is seen as a process, brain is the structure through which the process, in part, operates, and the nervous system, the immune system and the endocrine system form a single cognitive network.

Paul Maclean's definition of the evolutionary layering of the triune brain has provided a source of inspiration for the development of corresponding somatic tasks, to guide people through a movement experience of evolutionary states of being, and has also influenced Panksepp's argument that affective states, rooted in the older limbic brain, influence our behaviour more profoundly than our cognitive capacity. This positioning of affect is significant. Notions of the pervasive influence of affect are beginning to displace the more controlled information-processing models of cognition in daily life and neuroscience is moving towards a more spontaneous and sentient model of intelligence as it explores our feeling life. Affect has gained credence from neurobiological research such as Candace Pert's work in the field of neuropeptides, which has led her to see emotions as the link between mind and body – a link that is mediated by the neuropeptide system. She suggests that at a neurobiochemical level:

> We might refer to the whole system as a
> psychosomatic information network, linking
> psyche, which comprises all that is of an ostensibly
> nonmaterial nature, such as mind, emotion
> and soul, to soma, which is the material world
> of molecules, cells and organs. Mind and body,
> psyche and soma.

Even up to ten years ago, if an illness was referred to as psychosomatic, it was generally considered to be 'imagined' rather than 'real'. Here we see that, at a molecular level, neither mind nor body is 'real' in a situated sense, neither has a fixed place or position and that both fields are linked through core emotions which correspond to the neuropeptide system. All is in movement and change within the organism, responding to promptings from the limbic brain and influenced by neuropeptides. We shall see the significance of this as we consider the organism in the environment.

Lens 7: The Environmental Body

Session 4

We walk along shingle and sand at the sea's edge until we reach the big boulders revealed by the low tide. F. comments on how she needs to adapt her walking to the different surfaces and wants to take her shoes off. I suggest that she moves on the boulders, paying attention to how she places the palms of her hands, the soles of her feet and her sacrum. This gives a pattern of five points to pay attention to as she moves. As she moves, her body creates different shapes. Occasionally she pauses and feels her position in relation to the boulders, the sky, the sea and the cliffs. I notice that during this time she likes to wedge herself in cracks, fissures and crevices rather than to stay on top of the boulders.

She travels across the boulders but when she stops, it is in the cracks. Practice on the boulders requires her to look close in front for safety. Only when she stops can she lift her head and gaze into the distance. I ask her to try and let her eyes relax and to see if they can follow her movement, while she pays attention to the soundscape. As she becomes immersed in the rhythms of the wind, the waves and the birds, the rhythm of her own movement sequences begins to adapt and respond to the life around her. When she finishes, she finds a comfortable position, sitting on a boulder and rocking gently in the wind. She says that throughout the session she needed to move in the cracks to be aware of her body in the changing environment, to feel enclosed and safe. But in that last sitting position, she felt part of the situation, held by the rhythms of wind and sea. She felt a sense of her volume, position and her proportion in relation to both the molluscs and the towering cliffs. This moment of experience gave her the understanding that, if she took a photograph then, it would speak of her perception from within that moment not of her attempt to capture a moment from outside.

....

In conjunction with the previous definitions of body-mind (as seen through the lenses of phenomenology, somatics and neuroscience), which I shall refer to here as the body-mind-feeling life of the human organism, I now want to consider the Santiago theory of cognition, as developed by biological scientists Humberto Maturana and Francisco Varela. Speaking of interactions between organism (or autopoietic unity) and environment they say: 'the structure of the environment only triggers structural changes in the autopoietic unities (it does not specify or direct them) and vice-versa for the environment. [...] there will be a structural coupling'. This indicates a mutually dependent co-creation of any moment between the living system and its environment. A particular kind of terrain may trigger a certain kind of walk as a recurrent interaction, because of its physical characteristics and potential dangers, e.g. sharp rocks and the possibility of snakes. Changes are triggered at a structural level, but the organism is able to choose which triggers to respond to, certainly initially. Maturana and Varela propose:

> A way of seeing cognition not as a representation of the world 'out there', but rather as an ongoing bringing forth of a world through the process of living itself.

In the sessions, we see that F. has become aware of how new ways of moving in the boulders can 'bring forth' entirely new relationships with the environment. Afterwards, this experience stimulates her understanding (cognition) of previous habits and of her artistic process as a photographer.

With the Santiago theory we reach the threshold of the ecological body, as I am seeking to define it: a co-creating, immanent body, a body constantly becoming within a changing environment, where body and the spaces in between bodies are considered to be equally dynamic. But, for now, we stay with the environmental body. I would argue that it is primarily affect, rather than cognition, that conditions a living system's choice of which environmental triggers to respond to. Imagine an individual's body structure and how that has developed over time, influenced by genetic disposition and environmental factors. Imagine how that body engages with its environment (which it does through movement), in many different ways – which is what I am calling a body practice. Practice implies repetition until a particular pattern is integrated into the organism and into the environment. Such patterns may be unconsciously integrated or deliberately cultivated. They become what Paul Connerton calls 'incorporated' habits:

> Habits are more than technical abilities [...]
> All habits are affective dispositions [...] a
> predisposition, formed through the frequent
> repetition of a number of specific acts, is an
> intimate and fundamental part of ourselves.
> Postures and movements which are habit memories
> become sedimented into bodily conformation [...]
> Habit is not just a 'sign'. Habit is a knowledge and
> a remembering in the hands and in the body; and
> in the cultivation of habit it is our body which
> 'understands'.

Here Connerton suggests that a habit is an affective disposition, which seems likely, if we look, for example, at the power of addiction over rational intention. It may be that what specifies our response to triggers in the environment is our limbic brain, that is our affective life, rather than cognition, which would relate to the cortical brain.

As we have just seen, interaction with terrain may produce a particular style of walk which becomes incorporated as a habit. The practical function of the walk is forgotten, and it becomes the walk I use to cross any terrain, unless a new terrain is extreme enough to interrupt my habit and to allow the possibility of a new physical and affective response to my environment.

In my example, F. explores new movements that challenge her habits and change her perception. Her unfamiliar movements are 'disruptive' and open up new feelings, which in turn trigger a change in her understanding. I interpret the interactions of this living system with her environment as primarily kinaesthetic and affective, through a felt sense, rather than cognitive.

Moving in environments in ways that engage the whole body, such as crawling and rolling on the rocks, both opens up fresh perceptions of that place and challenges our habits, calling forth adaptability, flexibility and creativity. In order to develop skilfulness in movement, which would include the possibility of stepping outside ingrained habits, it is necessary to cultivate an awareness of how a moment is co-created between the body and a particular environment. This develops contextual awareness and makes sense of types of embodiment. Otherwise, if 'I' concentrate on training 'my body' as an isolated individual, not only am I training the body out of context and thus supporting an invalid belief, but also the influence of context, which could enable a greater sense of freedom or stimulate possibilities of transformation, is always missing from my awareness.

A consideration of environment is thus crucial both within subjective · movement practice and when witnessing the other in movement. In the same way as quoting someone out of context may serve to misrepresent them, so too, divorcing someone's movement from its particular context may lead to misrepresentation.

Lens 8: The Cultural Body

F. is moving with her colleague B. from Germany. B. moves in straight lines, and she often stops directly in front of F. and looks at her. She is moving confidently, briskly and succinctly, eyes open and looking horizontally, with clear definition in her finger movements. She does not appear to be aware of her back, or of the space behind her. Her approach to F. is very direct and uncompromising. Their pathways in movement keep missing each other in the hall.

Meanwhile, F. is moving in curves, circles and semi-circles, approaching and moving away from B. in equal measure. Her movement is slower and continuous, with few pauses. I can see that, although her eyes are open, she is paying more attention to her hearing than her vision. It is difficult for their pathways to meet. F. says that she feels confronted by B.'s directness and experiences it as 'bossy' and 'overpowering'. She feels like there is no room for her and wants to hide between cracks. B. says that she experiences F. as vague, as avoiding her or even as lying to her when she moves around. I suggest a little experiment: F. is to practise straight lines and to try and recall the feeling when she was sitting on the rock; B. is to practise moving from sounds and to practise crawling from time to time. This immediately changes her habitual relationship to straight lines and her rhythm. Slowly, their movement sequences find more points of contact and they begin to move in dialogue with each other.

....

Before engaging with the cultural body, and in order to place the significance of the body-in-movement-in-its-environment in a broader context, I turn to cultural historian Morris Berman's historical analysis of the displacement of the life of the body in favour of ideals. Berman's basic argument is that paradigm shifts arise when we have no sense of ground or of 'somatic anchoring' and that 'the human drama is first and foremost a somatic one'. One ideology, conditioned by the economic, social and philosophical needs of the time often replaces another as symptomatic relief from the deep discomfort of a sense of not belonging. Berman suggests that we need to examine the nature of paradigm itself, to look in the spaces between paradigms rather than from within them and to cultivate ways of becoming embodied to counteract this threat of 'the void'. Also, that we need to break the habit of creating an ideology as a substitute for facing up to our own profound discomfort and yearning. Only when we have faced and accepted this yearning can we hope to develop ways of being in the world that are congruent with embodied needs rather than abstract ideologies.

Berman traces this yearning developmentally. He relates it to an existential feeling of hollowness which he sees as emerging around our third year. At birth, we have no sense of ourselves as separate from the environment, but gradually, as we develop, we become aware of ourselves as separate, discrete entities with needs and desires. One key factor in this discovery of apparent isolation is the process of mirroring, the growth of self-recognition through the medium of other people.

> Self awareness is awareness of one's body as a
> separate entity, as a specular image [...] The self is
> a body self but gets elaborated in such a way as to
> take a viewpoint on the body, have a conception of
> it.

According to Berman, this results in the decision to distrust the evidence of our senses and we shift away from a kinaesthetic sense of being to a relationship with a visually based body image. Apart from this application of early developmental psychology and movement to historical analysis, which is in itself a fascinating testimony to the links between individual and cultural psychosomatic development and subsequent cultural identity, his analysis yields another area of enquiry.

He suggests that at any given period in a culture there will be a particular balance between the kinaesthetic and visual senses, just as there will be 'a typical ecology of personality that integrates the self/other, mind/body relationship in a particular way'. As an example of the above, he states that:

> Imperialism has at its root the interpretation of self
> by other, the imposition of a visual interpretation
> on an original kinaesthetic one. A colonized people
> intuitively knows this and that is why magic is
> frequently resorted to as a weapon: it is a tool for
> doing away with the visual interpretation and
> reinstalling the kinaesthetic one.

Looking somatically at imperialism as one intercultural mechanism, it becomes possible to use movement to identify, understand and, if necessary, transform ingrained cultural attitudes and tendencies, to shift deeply rooted 'incorporations' and to create new ways of moving forwards in dialogue with each other, whilst respecting diversity. Here, Berman identifies the polarity between visual and kinaesthetic modes of attention (as discussed in *Lens 1: The Body as Object*) as one of the root causes of imperialism.

It may be that the experience of self-validation in the body, created by 'matching' and 'guiding' (as described in *Lens 6: The Interdependent Body*), which are forms of embodied mirroring, reawakens a dormant kinaesthetic sense of being. In my own work, I apply cultural lenses to different movement dynamics, such as active/passive, transition/position, proportion and point, line and angle to reveal the somatic heritage of other habitual, cultural mechanisms. Establishing a self-reflexive, somatic approach to the dynamics underlying the attraction between Eastern and Western disciplines, for example, in an attempt to open a shared pathway of action and understanding, is a core aspect of my practice of cultural embodiment through movement.

As we have seen in F.'s session by the sea, by identifying a particular habit in movement in the environment, a participant can connect that pattern to ways in which they engage with areas of their daily life. According to Connerton: 'Bodily practices of a culturally specific kind entail a combination of cognitive and habit memory'. Affect, as he sees it, is at the root of habit. If I choose to look at movement through cultural lenses, trends of intercultural misunderstanding can be traced back to unconscious individual movement preferences, which we have unknowingly inherited through mimicking and which have then become habits: the way that a person moves through space, the way they hold themselves, or a particular relationship to time/rhythm that may hold an utterly different meaning in a different culture. In Connerton's eyes, an apparently similar cultural gesture, (which he calls a technique), can arise from different intentions:

> [...] the Southern Italians illustrate gesturally the objects of their mental acts as a lexicon which goes back historically, whereas European Jews produce gestural notation for the process of their mental activity, like musical scoring.

This observation takes us back to the practice of noticing whether someone's movement arises from physical sensations, from thought processes or from feelings, by paying attention to their relationship to context/environment: in this case, their cultural context.

Once these habits or trends have been brought to light, it is possible to play with alternative movements, as in the case study, and to see how a mutual, non-verbal situation of comprehension may be reached either between individuals or in a group. These discoveries can create shifts of attitude without compromise, which permit a more transparent dialogue between diverse cultures while respecting differences.

In non-stylised movement practice, the tasks and scores that people are invited to undertake may be practical, such as: 'Investigate how you move from lying down to standing'. They may revolve around the investigation of a particular dynamic, such as transition/position within particular environmental contexts. For example: 'Notice when you choose to cross the space, and when you choose to stay on the spot'. Either way, individuals witness their own approach to the task in the context of the way that others in the group are approaching the same instruction. The different emergent approaches may offer different, unexpected but distinct cultural, generational, or gendered resonances, to name but three possible observational maps. The experience of difference validates each person's unique approach without forfeiting a sense of communal endeavour.

Similarly, Martin Jackson points out that undertaking a practical task in another culture can often convey an embodied sense of that activity. The in-coming worker is doing the same thing as other bodies, but all are doing it in their own, culturally conditioned way. This, he says, is a creative technique that reveals both consonance and individual meaning. He sees these as ways of:

> ...opening up dialogue between people from
> different cultures or traditions, ways of bringing into
> being modes of understanding which effectively go
> beyond the intellectual conventions and political
> ideologies that circumscribe us all.

Undertaking physical tasks, whether based in daily-life activity or in non-stylised movement, seems to be an important, non-hierarchical way of giving presence to other-than-verbal experiences of each other's beings-in-the-environment, as a way of promoting 'holarchy', a recently coined term to indicate a human system, each element of which displays both self-assertive and integrative tendencies. Jackson argues that: 'Persons actively body-forth the world; their bodies are not passively shaped by or made to fit the world's purposes'. He does not see bodily behaviour as symbolising ideas conceived independently of it.

The notion of an ecological body implies that human beings interact with their environment and that human and environment co-create one another. In order to develop a sense of an ecological body, a body that experiences itself through movement as part of a changing environment, rather than as a static isolated individual, a crucial part of skills training is to engage in a dynamic and kinaesthetic dialogue with the environment. Environment and culture, in this approach, are inextricably linked and, as demonstrated above, are both present in the articulations of the moving body.

In cultural anthropology, Thomas Csordas defines embodiment as follows:

> Embodiment is an existential condition in
> which the body is the subjective source or
> intersubjective ground of experience. Therefore
> studies of embodiment are about culture and
> experience insofar as these can be understood
> from the standpoint of bodily being in the world
> [...] Embodiment is about experience and
> subjectivity and understanding these is a function
> of interpreting action in different modes and
> expression in different idioms rather than about
> behaviour or essence.

In relation to Csordas's analysis, I am suggesting that 'different modes' in movement could consist of activity, actions and acts (all based in movement) that are the embodiment of that particular mover. Each mode provides motion and physical sensations, with attention to oneself, to others and to the environment in varying proportion. There is no sign of any essential being, only a shifting range of expressive idioms. Movement training in the environment offers a training in contextual embodiment, when movers begin to bodily recognise and own their distinctive and particular environmental and cultural preferences within the context of a group. The group provides a self-reflexive and relational system for acknowledging differences, including the fact that, as observed by Csordas, 'the *deployment* of the senses and sensibility, not only (just) their content is emphatically cultural' (my italics).

Lens 9: The Ecological Body

F. and I walk down to a rock amphitheatre at the sea's edge, hewn out through a history of quarrying for stone.

I ask her to move from angles: angles that she creates through her body structure in movement, angles that she creates between her body and the environment and angles that she 'imitates' in the environment, or responds to through movement. I invite her to consider an angle of view and sound as an angle.

As F. starts to work with the task her habitual vocabulary is disrupted through her growing fascination with exploring this moving geometry. The angles encourage her to create sculptural shapes which often resonate with the shapes in the landscape around her. Her movement appears more incorporated into her surroundings and her attention is shifting on the threshold between her inner stories and her outer environment. At one moment, I can see from a change of expression and atmosphere that one of her articulated positions has connected with a somatic memory; at the same moment a gull screams overhead – a sharp, angular call – and glancing upwards, she follows the emergent sequence of movements without hesitation.

As she comes to rest, her autobiographical improvisation has led her into an angular niche within the towering rock face and crouching down she turns her back to the sea and shapes herself into the position of a breathing cornerstone.

I am quiet inside as a few words pass through my mind: the meeting of the ancestors...

....

Environmental movement training provides several tools that may be seen as developing 'somatic modes of attention'.

Matching and guiding are somatic modes of attention that refer to a moving situation and that pay attention to time. I describe an ecological body as a 'body-in-movement-in-a-changing-environment'. It is the emphasis on viewing the world through a lens of transition or flux, from movement and constant change, that distinguishes it in my mind from the 'environmental body', which is situated in a specific location and is in change but is often articulated as if viewed through a static lens.

In this book I have examined the 'situation' of the body through various lenses, in order to place my notion of an ecological body in context. Body and environment, I suggest, co-create each other through mutual influence and interactional shaping. The body-in-movement, as a relational body, sets up different practices through habit according to its intentions, perceptual life, experiences and cultural preferences. The ecological body is situated in movement itself and as a system dancing within systems, rather than as an isolated unit. So I finish by reflecting on aspects of movement in my practice that contribute to this notion of an ecological body.

The ecological body as a lens takes movement as the basic default, with 'stillness' or 'stopping' as pauses in the line of movement. Inspired by *Joged Amerta,* this is a key factor, offering a perception of the world that is utterly different from the one that we are generally accustomed to. Even in a fixed position there is still the movement of our breathing or of our circulation, so, in fact, like the rest of the natural world, we are constantly in change or in some kind of transition. In absolute terms, there is no such thing as a fixed 'position' because there is always movement.

However, within a comparative framework, the kinaesthetic emphasis in Western daily life is on one's position, on goals and on structure rather than paying attention to transition: that is to process, to the journey or to the spaces between activities. To redress the balance, I point to transition even though position is, itself, transition. If I take 'stopping' as the basic default, I may be unconsciously looking at life from the viewpoint of death, which is the only time we do, in fact, stop moving. A stopping point becomes the reference point for the sequence of movement preceding it. The tendency is to look back to see how someone can 'improve' what they just did. Taking 'change' as home ground suggests an approach to life that acknowledges the potential for transformation, or 'blossoming': a term used by Suryodarmo in *Joged Amerta*. In practical terms, this means that when I watch someone move, I am looking to support their full potential in movement, as it is happening, to expand their choices, rather than looking back to see what they cannot do.

Secondly, in my perception, movement is inextricably linked to the body, to the environment, to change and to the expression of life or being alive. It is a constant, a continuity that underlies the process of living and therefore difficult to define except, perhaps, by its absence. I have referred to evolutionary movement and to child developmental movement. These systems, based on neurobiology and psychology, correspond to the evolution of the species and the individual respectively. At the death of an organism, movement ceases.

Movement has traditionally been more connected to an image of the body than to an image of mind, and therefore suffers the same prejudices as the mechanistic body suffered through the postulation of a body-mind split: movement, in this dualistic context, has generally been seen as a vehicle for the expression of the mind/spirit. As a result of this prevalent attitude, movement becomes something we do rather than something we are. However, returning to my earlier distinction, there are practices that see movement from the point of view of the body and that see movement as inherently meaningful, rather than looking for the psychology or story that a movement sequence is revealing. When I listen to music, I am not necessarily seeking meaning, but nevertheless, in the process of listening, the music has meaning for me. It is the same with watching the moving body.

Third, my notion of the ecological body is based on the hypothesis that such a body perceives the moving world through movement and experiences itself as one part of a changing situation. As an ecological body engaged in ecological movement, I am aware of the effect that my movement is having on others and on the environment itself, and how they are conditioning my movement. Habitual characteristics and tendencies become apparent in my movement patterns: they are the movements which repeat themselves through changing environments. With awareness, I contend, these can be accepted and then transformed by adopting new movement preferences or releasing the tension of a particular pattern and seeing what movement arises.

Finally, by moving in natural environments, ecological movement helps people to expand their embodied awareness to include the broader context from a position of 'being among', rather than 'being central to'. From that position they may experience their own system as an intrinsic part of a wider set of systems and act accordingly, rather than perpetuating an attitude of 'using' the environment. Ecological dynamics, dynamics that touch certain nodal points, where human movement interrelates with the environment through time, are the foundation stone of ecological movement practice. These include active/passive, proportions in motion, transition/position and point, line and angle as ways of working. The intention is to foster an attitude of biocentric equality through movement, through embodied experiences of 'interbeing'. Biocentric equality is the notion that all things have an equal right to live and to fulfil their particular potential. By rediscovering the flow of environment, rather than the environment as a succession of places, and by challenging our addiction to 'doing' at the expense of our experiencing our 'being' in the world, there is a chance that we can give value to our selves and to our life stories as part of a profoundly interrelated network of beings.

An ecological body is situated in flux, participation and change. The changing body/soma experienced through movement as part of the changing environment challenges any fixed and deterministic notion of self and stimulates a different sense of self as process, participating in the movement of life.

Notes

p.1 – Time frame

In discussing the lenses that have been used in the West in the last few hundred years, I leave aside – but don't intend to discount or devalue – the approaches used at other times, in other cultures and in other parts of the world.

p.1 – Lenses

Even listing the different lenses is a kind of fragmentation, like that represented by, for example, those dualists who view the body as an object. But the intention in separating out these different lenses is simply to make them clear, rather than to suggest that each has an independent existence.

p.2 – Case study

This type of hypothetical case study is often found in anthropology. In creating it, I have combined and conflated movement sessions with different clients and changed individual details to make it completely anonymous. While much of my theoretical approach *has* been derived from my experience of moving and from my movement teaching and therapy practice, my intention here is purely illustrative: to show how the theory can be seen at work in our daily lives.

Notes

Lens 1

p.6 – Commodification

Wilkinson is writing in Wilkinson, Payne and Corrigall [2006: 87].

p.7 – Sight

The description of sight is taken from Daboo [2004: 24].

pp. 7-8 – The act of vision

The quotation is from Dewey [1930: 23].

p.8 – Individualism

For more on this notion of individualism, see Jackson [1989: 8] who cites Siegfried Giedion on the subject.

Lens 2

p.11 – Via negativa

'*via negativa* - not a collection of skills but an eradication of blocks' [Grotowski, 1975: 17].

p.11 – Phenomenology and somatics

These are the subject of the next two lenses and can be seen as different 'styles' of the Body as Subject.

p.12 – Body-mind debate

See Wilkinson, Payne and Corrigall [2006: 1].

p.12 – Neuroscience

See Panksepp [2006].

LENS 3

p.14 – Husserl

The opening quotation is from Jennings [1986: 1239].

p.14 – Self-image

See Feldenkrais [1980].

p.14 – Phenomenology

For more on this subject see, in particular Stevens [1996] and Merleau-Ponty [2002].

p.15 – Consciousness

The quotation is from Jennings [1986: 1238].

p.15 – Phenomenology of the lived body

The quotation is from Calvin Schrag cited in Zarrilli (1998).

pp. 15-16 – 'Meaning'

Technically, here, I am referring to noesis. Movement can evoke multiple noematic interpretations.

LENS 4

p.18 – Janet Eddy

The reference is to Eddy [2009:7]

p.18 – Somatic systems

On somatics, see Hanna [1988] and on BMC see Bonnie Bainbridge Cohen [1993].

p.19 – Somatic practice

For the material in the remainder of this lens, I have drawn on my own movement practice: *Move into Life*. The first training module, called 'Body in Movement', specifically uses a somatic approach and it is exercises from that module that I refer to here. 'Participants', therefore, refers to people (normally new to movement work) attending that module.

p.19 – Janet Kaylo

All references to her work on this page are drawn from Kaylo [2003].

p.19 – Laban

When I refer to movement, I am thinking of it in the terms defined by Rudolf Laban:

> The effort elements are attitudes of the moving person towards the motion factors Weight, Space, Time and Flow. The new dance-training fosters the development of a clear and precise feel of man's attitude towards his efforts.
> (Laban, 1948: 8)

Laban saw the effort elements as stimuli taking place before the visible movement, as well as reflected in the movement itself. Each element exists along a spectrum. Weight, for example, exists between light and heavy/strong thus allowing for a qualitative, nuanced analysis of a person's movement. Using the elements of effort to analyse both human and environmental movement can support the coherence of a training that encourages movers to feel themselves as part of the environment rather than separated from it.

p.21 – Averse, acquisitive, confused

In Buddhist teaching, this triad of *lobha* or greed, *dosa* or hatred and *moha* or delusion are seen as the basic *kilesas* or 'defilements'.

The choice of words, 'acquisitive', 'averse' or 'confused' honours the terminology given to the three possible types of feeling by John Garrie Rōshi (1924-1999) in his teaching of *Satipatthāna*.

LENS 5

p.24 – Authenticity

The quotation is from Johnson [1992: 155].

p.24 – Amanda Williamson

The quotations are from Williamson [2009:30].

p.25 – Bainbridge Cohen

The quotation is from Bainbridge Cohen [1993:1].

p.25 – Joged Amerta

Joged Amerta is a movement practice developed by Suprapto Suryodarmo, a Javanese movement artist whose intention is to 'lessen the sense of identification through the practice of movement arts'.

Amerta is a Javanese word which he translates as the 'nectar' or 'elixir' of life. This practice is founded on the basic movements of daily life: walking, sitting, standing, crawling and lying down and the transitions between them, beginning with the observation of children playing. It is also based on moving in nature and an embodied study of movement from the play of elements in motion and the laws of nature.

His work is described in Lavelle [2006], Bloom [2007], Reeve [2009] and elsewhere.

LENS 6

pp. 28-29 – Matching

The quotations are from Behnke writing in Johnson [1995: 325-326].

p.29 – Kinetic mirroring

The description of kinetic mirroring is taken from Hanna [1988: xiv].

p.30 – Interspecies dialogue

I explored dialogue between primates and performers in the Bristol Zoo project (*Being in Between*) that I co-directed in 2005. For more information, see Reeve [2009] or follow the link to my PhD Extracts at www.moveintolife.com and then to *Being in Between*.

p.30 – Guiding

In *Joged Amerta,* Suprapto's way of teaching movement through movement, (as well as through story and verbal instruction), by 'guiding' movers, which he does through moving, singing, making music and by paying attention to the atmosphere of a given situation, has radically influenced my approach.

p.31 – Neuroscience

For more on the convergence between body, mind and perception see Capra [1997].

p.31 – Paul Maclean

Maclean is referenced in Olsen [2000].

pp. 31-32 – Affect

On the influence of affect in daily life, see Thrift [2004].

p.32 – Candace Pert

The quotation comes from Pert [1999: 185].

LENS 7

p.34 – Autopoietic unity

Autopoiesis, a term used by Maturana and Varela, is the system that makes living beings autonomous systems. An 'autopoietic unity' is a single living organism. It is their organisation that defines them as unities. See Maturana and Varela [1987].

The quotations on this page are from Maturana and Varela [1987: 75 and 11].

p.35 – Habits

The quotation is from Connerton [1989: 75].

p.36 – Moving in the environment

This experience relates in particular to two modules of my training programme: 'Journey' explores a repeating journey from hilltop to sea over several days and 'Strata' invites participants engaged in environmental movement to explore an autobiographical theme.

LENS 8

pp. 40-41 – Morris Berman

See Berman [1989: 108 and 36]. The longer quotations are from Berman [1989: 166 and 168].

p.41 – Movement dynamics

For more on the movement dynamics of active/passive, transition/ position, proportion and point, line and angle, see Reeve [2009] or follow the link to my PhD Extracts at www.moveintolife.com and then to 'Movement Dynamics'.

p.42 – Cultural gestures

See Connerton [1989: 81].

p.43 – Tasks

I have chosen tasks from my own teaching practice, but others working in the tradition of Joged Amerta and other non-stylised movement approaches use very similar tasks.

p.43 – Martin Jackson

The extracts are from Jackson [1989: 3 and 136].

pp. 43-44 – Holarchy

For more on this topic see Leicester & O'Hara [2007].

pp. 44-45 – Thomas Csordas

The paragraph on embodiment and the final observation are taken from Csordas [1999: 143-155].

LENS 9

p.48 – Somatic modes of attention

This is a construct advocated by Thomas Csordas as one possible way of approaching embodied cultural phenomenology:

> Somatic modes of attention – culturally elaborated
> ways of attending to and with one's body in
> surroundings that include the embodied presence
> of others.
> (Csordas, 1993: 138)

p.48 – The situated body

In my readings of the 'situated' body, although change, movement and process are referenced throughout, I feel that this same distinction holds true: the primary lens through which the body is viewed remains static, as indicated by the choice of word 'situated'. See Ingar Brinck [2007], Dorothée Legrand [2007] and Shaun Gallagher [2007].

p.49 – Neurobiology and psychology

See Olsen [2000] and Bainbridge Cohen [1993].

p.50 – The inherent meaning of movement

Some of those practices and practitioners that see movement as inherently meaningful are discussed by Bainbridge Cohen [1993], Feldenkrais [1980], Gallagher [2007] and Hanna [1988].

p.50 – Nodal points

A nodal point is 'where most of a system's functions converge and where action would produce most change with the least effort', according to Mara Selvini Palazzoli *et al.*, cited in Boscolo and Bertrando [1993: 95].

p.50 – Interbeing

In a Western context, Merleau-Ponty, in a series of lectures called *The Concept of Nature*, explored the phenomenon of 'Ineinander' or 'in one another' (originating in the work of Edmund Husserl) and is quoted in an article by phenomenologist Will Adams as saying: 'the concern is to grasp humanity ...not as another substance, but as interbeing...' [Merleau-Ponty cited in Adams, 2007].

Bibliography

Adams, W. (2007) 'The Primacy of Interrelating', *The Journal of Phenomenological Psychology*, no. 38, pp. 24-61.

Bainbridge Cohen, B. (1993) *Sensing, Feeling and Action*, Northampton, MA: Contact Editions.

Berman, M. (1989) *Coming to our Senses: Body and Spirit in the Hidden History of the West*, New York: Simon and Schuster.

Bloom, K. (2006) The *Embodied Self: Movement and Psychoanalysis*, London: Karnac.

Boscolo, L. and Bertrando, P. (1993) *The Times of Time: A New Perspective in Systemic Therapy and Consultation*, New York: W.W. Norton & Co Inc.

Brinck, I (2007) 'Situated Cognition, Dynamic Systems, and Art: On Artistic Creativity and Aesthetic Experience', *Janus Head*, vol. 9, no.2, pp.407-431.

Capra, F. (1997) *The Web of Life*, London: Harper Collins.

Connerton, P. (1989) *How Societies Remember*, Cambridge: Cambridge University Press.

Daboo, J. (2004) *The Mind of a Flower – the psychophysical experience of performance*, PhD Thesis, University of Exeter, UK.

Dewey, J. (1930) *The Quest for Certainty: a study of the relation of knowledge and action*, London: Allen & Unwin.

Eddy, M. (2009) 'A brief history of somatic practices and dance: historical developments of the field of somatic education and its relationship to dance', *Journal of Dance and Somatic Practices*, vol. 1, no. 1, pp. 5-27.

Feldenkrais, M. (1980) *Awareness through Movement*, Harmondsworth: Penguin Books.

Gallagher, S. (2007) 'Introduction: The Arts and Sciences of the Situated Body', *Janus Head*, vol. 9, no. 2, pp. 293-295.

Grotowski, J. (1975) *Towards a Poor Theatre*, London: Methuen.

Hanna, T. (1988) *Somatics*, Cambridge, MA: Da Capo Press.

Jackson, M. (1989) *Path Towards a Clearing: Radical Empiricism and Ethnographic Enquiry*, Indiana: Indiana University Press.

Jennings, J. L. (1986) "Husserl Revisited: The Forgotten Distinction between Psychology and Phenomenology", *American Psychologist*, vol. 41, 1231-1240.

Johnson, D. H. (1992) *Body Recovering our Sensual Wisdom*, Berkeley, CA: North Atlantic Books.

Johnson, D. H. (ed.) (1995) *Bone, Breath and Gesture: Practices of Embodiment*, Berkeley, CA: North Atlantic Books.

Kaylo, J. (2003) Four day training in Laban Movement Analysis and Dance Movement Therapy Applications: class notes: March-May 2003: London.

Lavelle, L. (2006) *Amerta Movement of Java 1986-1997: An Asian Movement Improvisation*, Lund, Sweden: Centre for Languages and Literature, Lund University.

Legrand, D (2007) 'Pre-Reflective Self-Consciousness: On Being Bodily in the World', *Janus Head*, vol. 9, no. 2, pp. 493-519.

Leicester, G. and O'Hara, M. (2007) *Ten Things to do in a Conceptual Emergency*, Axminster: Triarchy Press.

Maturana, H. and Varela, F. (1987) *The Tree Of Knowledge: The Biological Roots of Human Understanding*, Boston, MA: Shambala Publications.

Merleau-Ponty, M. (2002) *Phenomenology of Perception*, Oxford: Routledge.

Olsen, A. (2000) *Body and Earth*, NY: University Press of New England.

Panksepp, J. (2006) 'The core emotional systems of the mammalian brain' in Wilkinson, H., Payne, H. and Corrigall, J. (2006).

Pert, C. (1999) *Molecules of Emotion*, London: Pocket Books.

Reeve, S. (2009) *The Ecological Body*, PhD Thesis, University of Exeter, UK

Stevens, R. (1996) *Understanding the Self*, London: Sage Publications

Thrift, N. (2004) 'Intensities of Feeling: Towards a Spatial Politics of Affect', *Geografiska Annaler*, 86B (1), pp. 57-78.

Wilkinson, H., Payne, H. and Corrigall, J. (eds.) (2006) *About a Body: Working with the Embodied Mind in Psychotherapy*, London: Routledge.

Williamson, A. (2009) 'Formative Support and Connection: Somatic movement dance education in community and client practice', *Journal of Dance and Somatic Practices*, vol. 1, no. 1, pp. 29-45.

Zarrilli, P.B. (1998) *When the Body Becomes All Eyes*, New Delhi: Oxford University Press.

About the Author

Dr. Sandra Reeve is a movement teacher, artist, director and movement psychotherapist, offering therapy and supervision in private practice. She lives in West Dorset.

Since 1999, she has taught an annual programme of autobiographical and environmental movement workshops called Move into Life and she creates occasional, small-scale ecological performances.

She is an Honorary Fellow at the University of Exeter.

www.moveintolife.com

Also in the series: *Ways of Being a Body*

Volume 2: Body and Performance

12 contemporary approaches to the human body that are being used by performers or in the context of performance training.

All 12 approaches represent the praxis and research of their authors. The chapters reveal a wide variety of different interests but they share the common framework of the notion of 'body as flux', of 'no fixed or determined sense of self' and of supporting the performer's being-becoming-being as a skilful creative entity, emphasising the intelligence of the body at work.

Volume 3: Body and Awareness

20 contemporary approaches to the study and experience of embodied awareness

The field of embodied awareness is transdisciplinary and multi-faceted: it has no academic subject listing, but is of central importance to those seeking to understand art, dance, the psychology of health, trauma, learning & development, the psycho-ecology of extinction and climate change, proprioception and interoception, ecological awareness, meditation, and the need for societal transformation in an age of multiple convergent crises. Here international practitioners bring a wide range of perspectives to the subject.

tp

About the Publisher

Triarchy Press is a Systems Thinking publisher of authors, books and ideas that remind us to be aware of the world around us in all its layered complexity. This awareness of the wider context, and of systemic interactions, underpins each of the overlapping subject areas in which we publish:

- Government, Education, Health and other public services
- Ecology, Sustainability and Regenerative Cultures
- Leading and Managing Organisations
- The Money System
- Psychotherapy and Arts and other Expressive Therapies
- Walking, Psychogeography and Mythogeography
- Movement and Somatics
- Innovation
- The Future and Future Studies

For more information about Triarchy Press please visit
www.triarchypress.net

tp

Lightning Source UK Ltd.
Milton Keynes UK
UKHW051508100622
404112UK00014B/431

9 781908 009326